THE SEASONS *&* THE FARMER
By F. Fraser Darling

THE SEASONS *&* THE GARDENER
By H. E. Bates

THE SEASONS *&* THE WOODMAN
By D. H. Chapman

THE SEASONS *&* THE FISHERMAN
By F. Fraser Darling

Each book illustrated with fifty drawings
by *C. F. Tunnicliffe, R.E., A.R.C.A.*

THE SEASONS
&
THE FISHERMAN

Wha'll buy caller herrin'?
They're bonnie fish and halesome farin',
Wha'll buy caller herrin',
New drawn frae the Forth?

When ye were sleepin' on your pillows,
Dreamt ye ought o' our puir fellows
Darkling as they faced the billows,
A' to fill the woven willows?

Buy my caller herrin',
They're no' brought here wi'out brave darin',
Buy my caller herrin',
Ye little ken their worth.

Wha'll buy my caller herrin'?
O ye may ca' them vulgar farin',
Wives and mithers, maist despairing,
Ca' them lives o' men.

Caller herrin'!

LADY NAIRNE

THE SEASONS & THE FISHERMAN

A Book for Children written by
F. FRASER DARLING *and illustrated*
with drawings by C. F. TUNNICLIFFE

CAMBRIDGE: AT THE UNIVERSITY PRESS, 1941

CAMBRIDGE UNIVERSITY PRESS

Cambridge, New York, Melbourne, Madrid, Cape Town, Singapore,
São Paulo, Delhi, Dubai, Tokyo, Mexico City

Cambridge University Press
The Edinburgh Building, Cambridge CB2 8RU, UK

Published in the United States of America by Cambridge University Press, New York

www.cambridge.org
Information on this title: www.cambridge.org/9780521175944

First published 1941
First paperback edition 2010

A catalogue record for this publication is available from the British Library

ISBN 978-0-521-17594-4 Paperback

CONTENTS

DEDICATION & PREFACE

Dear Alice and Adam,

When I began writing this book with thoughts of you and other children in my mind, I was full of the beauty and wonder of the sea, and of the country of the sea's edge. All my first chapter was about the sea and its movements, of the tiny life of the sea which helps to build up the larger creatures we know, and of the vast influence of the sea and its wealth on the lives of men. The fishermen were constantly in my mind; kindly, simple folk, and yet of great skill in their work; enduring of hardship and facing bravely the dangers of the sea which are never far away. I thought it a grand tale to tell—and so it is; but as I went on unfolding it for you truthfully, it seemed to me that much of this story of the fisherman was one of killing and death, things which we do not like. You and I and the rest of people have to get this straightened out in our minds: we shall not understand the world better by refusing to learn from such things. The fisherman is a hunter, and all catching of food by hunting means some cruelty somewhere, sometime, and some waste which cannot be avoided. The farmer grows many crops which please our senses of sight and smell as they grow, but most of his crops are grown for his animals to eat, and what does he do with his animals? All the sheep in Britain are kept first and foremost for mutton; the wool is of secondary importance. There is nothing good to be gained by our refusing to take pleasure in the yearly joy of the lambing season just because those lambs are born to be killed. Dairy cows are killed when their time of usefulness is over; were it not so the country would become full of old beasts, and food would be scarce for both young and old. Pigs

vii

are kept for no other end than for human food. But farming itself is concerned with the growth of living things and it is easy to write a book on this beauty of growth without mention of death. The mighty sea grows the fish and the whales, and the fisherman takes no part in that. He comes to take toll of that which Nature has grown, and therefore he comes to kill.

We must try not to feel sorrow for the individual animals which are killed for, after all, we all take life in some way or other. If we spray rose trees to get rid of green fly we feel no sorrow, yet those insects must feel discomfort in being sprayed, even if they do not feel pain in the same way that we do. The insects die, the rose lives. It is better to make up our minds that we have to take toll of living things, and not to shrink from what that means. But our plain duty is to think of the stocks of animals as a whole; it is over-fishing the seas or hunting whales to extinction or killing for fun that is truly cruel. We must not shrink from taking life, but let us take it with due care and build up the stocks from which we take it. The herring and the whale have the same right to their existence as a kind as have human beings, and each one of us has some responsibility for them. So let us enjoy the story of the fisherman and the life of the sea through the seasons.

F. F. D.

September, 1941
Isle of Tanera
Ross & Cromarty
Scotland

THE SEASONS
&
THE FISHERMAN

THE WATERS AND THEIR DENIZENS

THE PRIMEVAL OCEAN

THOSE men who have most knowledge about the ancient history of this globe or earth upon which we live tell us that life began in the oceans which were warm and soupy, two thousand million years ago. The rocks of to-day, from which we gain many facts of the life that was throughout the ages, give us no clues as to the nature and appearance of the earliest forms of life: tiny, formless specks of jelly left no skeletons or shells to be preserved in that early mud which has now become hard rock, much changed through heat and pressure.

The dark and soupy oceans have gone, and apart from such events as the earth becoming cooler and the air gathering more oxygen, living things themselves must have helped to make the waters of the earth as they are to-day. And how varied are these waters! Think of those you know yourself—the salt sea where the herring lives, the stagnant pools of the frogs and water beetles, the muddy rivers moving slowly towards the sea and the clear mountain streams where the trout lie in wait for the flies that have themselves spent their early life in the water.

The earliest living things were plants and their simpler forerunners, and these seaweed-like plants of the primeval oceans made the waters and the air fit for the later development of animals. The plants fed on the salts dissolved in the waters and formed starch in their fronds and stalks with the help of sunlight. When the animals came they fed on the plants, and it was not much later in this unfolding or evolution of living things that animals developed which ate some of the plant-eating animals.

The Waters of To-day

The oceans, inland seas, lakes, rivers and ponds of to-day are in-habited by living forms much less numerous than those which live on dry land, but which are as varied in their ways of life. I explained in an earlier book how man came to grow plants for himself and to keep animals, and thus became a farmer. His farm animals were of the grazing kind which could turn grass into milk, wool, meat or, as in the horse, into the power to do work. So far man has not farmed the oceans and large tracts of fresh water, though the day may come when he will, but in relation to the life of the seas he has remained a hunter, catching many kinds of fish and other animals by dint of his cleverness and hard work. He takes from the waters animals which have, as it were, grazed on smaller forms of life. Man fishes the seas for animals as small as the shrimp and as large as the blue whale, which is the biggest animal in the world. He fishes with fine net and coarse net, drift net and trawl net, with hooks of many sizes, with a harpoon or barbed spear which is shot from a gun, and his fishing takes him to all the seas of the world.

Diatoms

2

The Pastures of the Sea

Let us think for a moment of the life which forms what may be called the pastures of the seas and what animals are the gatherers of this wealth. The surface of the sea is peopled by millions and millions of microscopic plants called *diatoms* and *flagellates*. Diatoms can do nothing but float, but the flagellates, as their name tells you, have whip-like tails which allow them some movement by their own efforts. They have some of the characteristics of simple animals, but as they have the green pigment chlorophyll in their bodies and are thus able to build up starchy substance with the help of light, they are classed as plants.

These minute plants float by reason of being so small and having a large surface in relation to their weight. You might not thank me for explaining exactly why things with large surfaces in relation to weight do float easier, but you can determine the fact for yourself with a piece of silver paper which, if laid on water, will take a long time to sink. But if you screw that silver paper into a very tight ball, so that no air is enclosed, thereby lessening its surface area, and drop it into the water, it will sink immediately.

It is most important for the diatoms that they should remain in the surface layer of the sea because, being plants, they must have light in order to build up their tiny bodies. If diatoms sink more than a few fathoms they die and fall more quickly to the floor of the sea. (Those who follow the sea use the fathom as a unit for measuring depth, just as landsmen use the foot for measuring height and the yard for length. A fathom is six feet.) The microscopic plants of the sea, then, are gathering light and using some of the salts dissolved in the sea water in order to live and reproduce.

Flagellates

3

Tiny animals, many of them still too small to be seen with the naked eye, live on the diatoms and flagellates or whip-tails. They belong to a group known as the *copepods*, or water fleas, though they are not really fleas at all: it is their shape and quick sort of movement that are flea-like. Beds of mussels, cockles and oysters are also living on the diatoms, not by catching them as the jumping copepods do, but by straining the water through their feeding valves.

Copepods

The drifting life of the surface layer of the sea, whether diatoms, copepods or other tiny animals that have only very limited means of moving about, is called *plankton*, a word of Greek origin meaning that which drifts. It is a short and easy word and as it is the one generally used by scientists we might as well go on using it in this book. Plankton forms the meadows and pastures of the sea, the basis of every kind of fishery.

If you wish to make this plankton more real to your understanding, you might tow a cone-shaped net of fine silk through the sea for some way and then place a little of the slimy substance gathered on the silk on to a piece of glass with a drop of water, and examine it under the low power of a microscope. Fresh water has plankton also, particu-larly in still ponds and lakes, so if you cannot reach the sea you still have the chance to see the copepods—if you can find somebody to help you look through a microscope.

The diatoms will be seen as objects of varied and beautiful regular patterns, the copepods will be moving hither and thither springily and you may see the larval stages of crabs and marine worms there also. 'Larval' means the very young stage of some animals after hatching from the egg; the caterpillar is the larva of the moth or

4

butterfly, and just as these two are very unlike, so are the larvae of crabs and some other sea animals quite unlike the grown-up ones. One such wonderful glimpse through a microscope will tell you more surely than all the words and books that the waves we see breaking on the shore are not just so much water and sea salt, but a vast country of living things.

The plankton pastures of the sea have their seasons as marked as the meadows of the farm. Some creatures of the plankton appear later in the year than others and make for a succession of food material for larger animals of the sea, just as I told you in *The Seasons and the Farmer* that some grasses were earlier in the year than others. The sea off British shores is barest of plankton in January; there is a great surge of the growth of diatoms in the spring, followed by a swarming of copepods and other animal plankton. Sometimes in late May the sea may appear milky with the crowded microscopic and just-to-be-seen life of that season. My wife makes butter from the cream of our cows and we live so near the sea on our little island that when she wishes to put the butter in brine before patting it up, she goes down to the sea's edge and brings back a pail of salt water: but she cannot do this in May, June and July, for some kinds of water fleas which can be seen with the naked eye are then very numerous and it would hardly do to fill the butter with these specks of life. The quantity of plankton diminishes during late summer and autumn.

We know that on the farm several facts bring about the growth of grass in spring. One is the rise in temperature to a level which allows a plant to grow and which hastens chemical action in the soil to make more plant food available; another is the increase in the amount of light. These and similar facts influence the growth of the plankton, but in different ways. For example, the great storms of winter stir up the sand and mud of the sea floor and some of the soluble salts of calcium, phosphorus and nitrogen (do you remember my mentioning these as plant foods in *The Seasons and the Farmer*?) become dissolved in the sea water. Now the coldness of winter has also lowered the temperature of the surface water of the sea by several degrees, to a lower temperature than the water which has become newly charged with salts from the floor of the sea. You may have learnt in science lessons at school that a cubic centimetre of water weighs one gramme at a temperature of 4° Centigrade. An equal volume of water at a higher temperature will not weigh as much. So when the surface water of the sea is chilled in winter to a greater coldness than the water below, it naturally sinks because it is heavier, while water newly charged with salts necessary for plant growth rises to the surface. The diatoms, therefore, in the increasing light of spring find an immense store of food in the sea in the form of these salts of calcium, phosphorus and nitrogen. The first two substances go to form bone or shell of the animals that eat the plankton, and the last one goes to form muscle.

You will know if you have tried bathing in the spring that the water is still rather cold, and this is the condition preferred by the diatoms and plankton living on them. Too high a temperature prevents their growth, and thus it is that in the colder latitudes of the northern and southern temperate zones of the seas the growth of plankton is greatest. It is not by mere chance, then, that the great fisheries of the world are within these zones.

Food Chains

None of the true fishes caught by man can feed directly on the diatoms, for they are much too small to be sieved through the straining arrangements which the fishes have in their gills or throat. But many of them can feed on the copepods which eat the diatoms. Some fishes feed on smaller fish which eat the copepods and so we find that the society or economy of the sea is built up of a series of what are called *food chains*. The biologist, the man who studies the science of life, traces the links in these chains in great detail for the sake of discovery, but the fisherman has learnt through the ages the main character of food chains in the pursuit of his arduous calling. The fisherman is often able to help the biologist and now the biologist is finding facts by which he can directly help the fisherman.

Here is an example: the plant plankton of the sea sometimes increases to an enormous extent and makes the water a brownish green and sharp to the smell. The herring shoals do not like water in this state and the fishermen never shoot their nets in such a place—'baccy juice', they call it! But the herrings feed heavily on copepods, though when this animal plankton is abundant is not always clear to the naked eye. A scientist invented an instrument called a plankton indicator. It is towed behind the herring drifter for a little way and a silk filter is then examined: if it has been discoloured brown or green, the skipper knows that plant plankton is too abundant and he goes a few miles farther and tests again. If copepods are reasonably plentiful he shoots his nets in the fair hope that the shoals of herring will be feeding there.

Marine biologists, the men who study the life of the sea, are able to forecast the appearance and migrations of shoals of fish, their scarcity or plenty, through a detailed study of food chains in various parts of the seas, and we may be sure, as time goes on, the fisherman and scientist will become as good friends and as dependent on one another as are the farmer and agricultural scientists.

You would think that the largest fishes and animals of the seas which are at the top of the food chains would be feeding on fishes of considerable size. But that is not always so. The food chain may be a very short one and not nearly so difficult to understand as for a much smaller fish. For example, that largest of all the fishes, the basking shark or sail fish which we see in northern waters in summer, feeds on animal plankton directly. The great fish of thirty feet in length takes gulps of water through its wide mouth and presses it out

7

again through the fine sieves of its several gill slits. The plankton is left behind and swallowed. The blue whale of the Antarctic seas feeds on immense shoals of small crustaceans known to the whaling men as *krill*. The krill have fed directly on the plankton and now, taken into the whale's mouth, they are sieved from the water by the baleen plates which take the place of teeth in these whales. (The group of animals known as the Crustacea include the crab, lobster, shrimp, prawn and many others: the copepods themselves are very small crustaceans.)

The Shallows and the Deeps

The sea varies in depth just as the land varies in height, but it is in the surface waters, or where there is no great depth, that most of the life of the sea is to be found. The fisherman is not greatly interested in the water below two hundred fathoms because most of the fish we eat are found above that depth. Nevertheless, there are fish of special kinds, usually extremely ferocious ones, to be found in the very deep waters of the seas. They are ferocious because food is scarce down there and they have to be ready to tackle fishes bigger than themselves and swallow them whole. I know this sounds impossible, but it is true; the jaws of these fish can open extremely wide and their stomachs stretch. Intervals between meals are long!

A deep-sea fish

One of the reasons for the growing scarcity of life in the sea at the deeper levels is that light does not penetrate farther than about a hundred fathoms, and we know that light is essential for the growth of plankton. The life at each level of the sea below where plants can live must be dependent largely on what sinks from above in the way of dead stuff. There is a constant rain of dead plankton and larger animals falling to the bottom of the sea, but the lower levels have only the leavings and dead bodies of the layer above, and, as I say, those fish which are to be found very deep in the sea are ferocious.

I have tried in this short account to show you the sea as a home of living things, each of which may have its special relation to the others; but I have not tried to give you a list or a description of the many forms of creatures to be found in the fishing levels of the sea or which you may find on the seashore and in rock pools, because this would take us too far from the fisherman and his work. He is interested much more in the sea as a home of living things, the place where fish grow.

The Tides

The inshore fisherman is much influenced in his work by the movements of the tides and sometimes a fishery in a large sea may be affected by them. The sea rises and falls on a shore nearly twice every twenty-four hours. I say nearly because each tide takes about twelve hours and twenty-three minutes to rise and fall. Thus, as you have probably noticed yourselves while on holiday at the seaside, the high tide each day is about three-quarters of an hour later than it was the day before. There are some places where, as a result of their geographical position, the tides do not follow this normal rhythm: for example, Southampton Water has four tides a day because of the effect of the Isle of Wight forming the two channels of the Solent and Spithead, each bringing an inrush of water towards Southampton at different times of day.

If you look at a beach of shingle or sand sloping gently to the sea you will notice several high-tide marks where seaweed and driftwood have been cast by the waves. You would see by noting the high-tide mark each day that it was either coming progressively a little higher or lower than the day before. If you stayed up late enough each night to see the state of the moon, you would find that a day or two after new moon and full moon the tides came higher and receded lower than on other days, that these big tides of the new moon were a little bigger than were those at the full moon, and that the spring tides as they are called were biggest of all at the equinoxes—March and September. After the springs the tides reach a little lower down the beach for seven days until the moon is at its first or third quarter,

Tide marks on the beach

then it begins to come a little higher each day until the springs. The small tides are called neap tides.

The reason for the relation of the tides to the state of the moon is that the moon exerts a pull on the surface of the earth as it passes round it. The same pull is being made on the land as on the sea, but the land is solid and more able to resist the pull. Water is heavy, after all, and the moon can do no more than pull the seas hither and thither a few feet twice each day.

Each part of the coast has its special time for the high spring tides and this time is always the same. Here in the Anchorage of the Isle of Tanera where I live the high spring tide after the new and full moon is at 7.35 o'clock. We think this a very convenient time, for if it should blow a gale when the tide is very high we can keep an eye on the boats moored alongside our pier, and go to bed knowing there will be no high tide again before we are up in the morning. But when I went to Berwick some months ago, I found the tides almost the reverse of ours at home. The high springs were at 2.30 o'clock.

What is the height of a tide? This varies also from place to place. Here at Tanera the spring tide is given on the chart made by the British Admiralty as being 14 feet 3 inches, and the average height of a tide about British shores is between ten and twenty feet. There are such extremes as only four feet near the Mull of Cantyre and as much as forty feet at a place in Jersey. Once more the shape of the coastline influences the tides, this time their height. The mid-ocean tides are only five feet high.

The shape of the coast and the changing currents made by the daily rhythm of the tides affect the fish in their feeding. Perhaps the presence of a current or a calm will cause the fish food to be out and about where the fish can catch it, and if fishermen are using baited hooks this is the time fish are likely to be caught. Again, there may be a sunken rock in the path of a current where fish may usually be caught at the neap tides, but when the tides are at the springs the current will be too strong for the fish and they will not be swimming freely round the rocks. The fisherman, then, takes careful note of the state of the tides in the pursuit of his calling.

Light and Dark

The plankton is composed, as you have seen, of many forms. The diatoms float in the surface layers of the water and the several kinds of copepods, crab larvae and so on change the depth at which they live according to the amount of light reaching the surface. A bright day in June will send them down to about ten or fifteen fathoms, and then at night time they will be up at the surface, it being a general but not invariable rule that the animal plankton tends to rise nearer the surface of the sea in the evening. So it is easy to understand that the fish will be nearer the surface in the evening, following the copepods upwards in order to feed on them. The fisherman knows this and that the fish are ready to feed in the evening, and he may make large catches at that time. The herring drift nets are shot at night and hang as a forty-five foot screen below the surface, where the herring are busy feeding on the copepods. The fish would probably have swum under them had the nets been shot during the day.

Each kind of fishing needs special knowledge of the habits of the fish, whether herring, mackerel or saithe, or bottom feeders like the haddock, cod and flat fish such as plaice, soles and turbot, or shell fish like lobsters and crabs. The fisherman is a good naturalist.

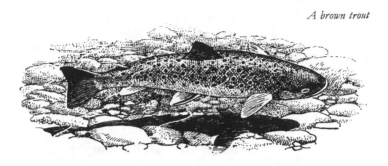

A brown trout

THE FRESH WATERS AND BEYOND

THE BROWN TROUT OF THE STREAMS

HAVE you ever watched a pool at the foot of a sparkling run in a small river? The water, often falling merrily over the stones, goes suddenly quiet and makes a foam-topped eddy before going on again down the path of the river. You may see a fly drop on to the surface of this pool, be whisked round by the eddy and before you can say Jack Robinson there is a slight ruffle of the water and the fly has gone. In that pool there was a brown trout and he was lying there waiting for such unfortunate flies or for food which might be brought down in that sparkling run.

Trout in Britain are not the subject of commercial fishery in the same sense as salmon or the herring and white fish of the open seas, though much money changes hands in the way of rents for rivers and payments for single days for the right to fish. Trout are fished for sport in this sense: if you merely wish to catch large numbers of trout they could be netted fairly easily, but the fisherman prefers to fish for individual trout with a light flexible rod, fine line, a still finer cast of

13

catgut and a tiny hook. The trout may not take that hook and if he does he may still free himself by swift movements or break the cast by hitching it round such obstacles as stones, weeds or tree roots in the river's bed.

The fisherman confines himself almost wholly to fishing for trout with tiny hooks dressed with wisps of feather to look like flies. Flies are creatures of spring and summer and thus we find that the trout fishing season extends only from 15 March to 15 October, and in many places, especially in Scotland, there are not many trout to be caught before May time or after the end of September. Some of these

Salmon and trout flies

dressed hooks may look like flies when dry, but when the fisherman makes his cast on to the water and the fly slowly sinks, its wings of feather fall in to the body and it looks more like the larval or pupal underwater form of the fly (sometimes called the nymph).

As we shall see later, the sportsman fishing for salmon in the rivers also uses a fly at the end of his line. The actions of fishing look much the same: the man draws back his rod with a deft movement of his wrist, the tip of it and the line and cast go up and backwards, and then he brings the rod forwards and downwards rather more gently, and if he is expert the line will run quietly along the surface of the water and the fly and hook drop without any splash or sound. But there is this very big difference between fly fishing for salmon and for trout. The salmon fisher's flies are like no fly you ever saw. The larger hook is dressed with feathers to make a thing which is brilliant to look upon—bright yellows, reds and blues, and silver tinsel. The flies used in Irish rivers are even larger and more brilliant than those used in England and Scotland. And we know that the salmon does not feed in fresh water, so the fish does not take as food these brilliant lures which hardly deserve the name of flies. I believe the salmon gets angry with the bright thing constantly crossing the surface of the water just above his head and—whoof!—he snaps at it. If I am right then, the clever salmon fisherman is he who can annoy the fish most thoroughly without frightening it.

The art of the trout fisher is much more delicate. His flies are made to imitate real flies or larvae as closely as possible, and some of them are very small. And when he makes his cast he must do it so well that his artificial fly falls on the water as quietly as a real fly might. He is imitating the food of the fish and presenting it to him as if it were food.

Once the fish has taken the dressed hook, the task of the fisherman is much the same, whether it is salmon or trout. Each fish swims away wildly and takes a great length of line from the reel at the base of the rod. The fisherman must allow the fish to run and not let it put too much strain on the fine tip of his rod. The salmon usually makes a bigger fight than a trout and it is not unusual for a fisherman to be trying for an hour to work a salmon close enough to be brought ashore. The fish gradually exhausts itself by these wild runs and can then be wound in by the fisherman and taken from the water without fear of breaking the line.

The trout fisher must know much more of the natural history of the river he is fishing than the salmon fisher needs to know. He must find out exactly what sort of flies are hatching and when they hatch, so that he may make his own cast in the guise of food for the trout.

15

The trout of different rivers bite more readily on different kinds of artificial fly, and flies must be altered with changes in weather, the season and the amount of water going down the river.

The trout fishers of the chalk streams of England have learned to fish even more delicately than ordinary fly-fishers. They use what is called a dry fly. When a common artificial trout fly falls on the water it tends to sink as soon as the feathers get wet and the weight of line and cast draw it down. The dry-fly man greases his line and cast so that they do not sink and the flies are very small and beautifully made. He uses a very light rod and you may

Fly-fishing for trout

see him of a summer's evening fishing at exactly the right moment when the fish are beginning to rise and make little circular ripples on the smooth surface of the water. The dry-fly fisher is a quiet man; he may be kneeling on one knee, his fine rod plays above his head and out along the water runs the greased line without so much as a ripple; and there floats his tiny fly looking no different from the real ones. This is a different kind of fishing indeed from the heavy gear of the North Sea trawlers working through a winter's night.

Sometimes the trout fisher may put by his flies and use a worm on his hook, for there are some trout that will not take a fly. They are usually large, old fish that dominate a deep pool. In Highland streams where I have done most of my trout fishing I have found that a deep pool at the foot of a waterfall often holds one of these old fish which will never come from the depths for a fly. His normal meals consist of wormy food coming down the fall and of small trout which he can catch by a sudden snatch. When brought ashore these fish have none of the beauty of the younger, more active trout of shallower water. They are dark in colour and their heads are large in relation to their bodies. They look what they are—cannibals.

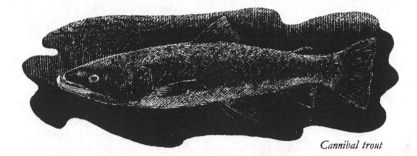

Cannibal trout

The trout streams of England are strictly preserved and the sportsman pays heavily for his fishing. Scotland is more fortunate; there is no law to prevent anyone fishing for brown trout in a river or stream, but if you wish to fish it is customary and polite to ask the owner of the river bank for permission, and it is rarely withheld.

If you fish for trout when you are young, you come to know the country round you in a rather special way. You learn the watercourses thoroughly, you learn the depths and forces of them as you would in no other way, and you get to know well the natural history of river banks. How common are alder and willow trees there! We find the tracks of water voles, brown rats and otters, and weasels and stoats often enough, for a stream is a highway for animals just as a large river is for men. I remember once when I was very small leaving fishing for a whole afternoon because I had crept to the bank of the stream on my hands and knees, and there below me on a tiny beach of gravel was a family of water shrews playing games. Never since have I been lucky enough to watch these shy animals for so long, just a foot away from my nose.

The birds of the river are characteristic also. You may see the kingfisher flash to and fro; or, if you live in the north, the cheerful, white-breasted dipper which is the only aquatic bird with a song, and a song which he sings even in winter. There is more than the song of the dipper for you to enjoy. The paired birds often dance a pretty little measure in which they appear to curtsey to each other several times. Sometimes you will see a heron standing motionless on the bank, waiting for a trout or eel to come near. If you are lucky again not to be seen by him, it is possible he may pass his beak through his breast feathers where they are very scaly and powdery. By this means he roughens

Duck and drake mergansers

the inside of his beak and makes it easier to hold such a slippery fish as an eel when he catches it. If you live in the north a red-breasted merganser may be seen fishing by diving. The bill of this bird needs no powdery feathers to roughen it, because the edges are like a saw and hold a fish easily.

The good trout fisherman is one who does not grow downhearted if he catches no fish, for he has besides the whole of the life of the river and its banks to enjoy.

18

The Ocean-going Sea Trout

Many fish are unable to withstand marked changes in their *environment* or set of conditions in which they live, and this fact, together with that of the restricted range of some fish food, enables the fisherman to go forth on such an immense area as the sea and catch fish with a fair degree of certainty. He knows the haddock feeds on the sea floor and at some seasons prefers places where the bottom is twenty to thirty fathoms deep. He knows these banks and takes his boat straight there. Fish generally are either of the sea or of the fresh water, and a

A hooked sea-trout

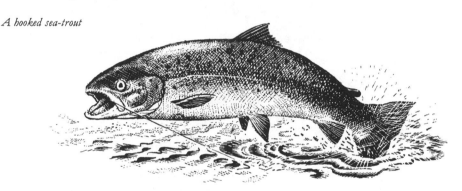

change from one to the other would kill them. The great sturgeon and the tiny stickleback, the salmon and sea trout are exceptions to this rule, and the sea trout particularly is an interesting fish because it is able to live in salt, fresh or brackish water, and changes its environment often in the course of its life—but strangest of all, the sea trout and the brown trout are the same species of animal.

Let us try to get this point right in our minds: the trout is a fish which can inhabit several kinds of environment, but by doing this the trout finds himself changed into two or three different types of fish according to the conditions in which he lives. It is as if you became an Eskimo if you were to go to Greenland or a Negro if you went to West Africa, and changed back to being a Briton when you came home. In earlier days fishermen thought these several kinds of trout were different species entirely: for example, there was the brown trout so well known in fresh water, the sea trout, the cannibal trout which they call *ferox*, and the slob trout which lives continually in estuaries. Now we know these are all trout, just changed by living in different places.

The brown trout, born and grown in the fresh water of the streams and lakes, stays there; some may go down to the estuary to become slob trout, but it is unusual for them to take fully to the open sea. The sea trout is born in the streams just as is his brother, but at the age of from two to four years, when he looks exactly the same as a brown trout, he begins a journey towards the sea. He is then called a *smolt*, and is found to be developing a silveriness of the skin. Once that silveriness is complete he takes to the sea and feeds there, travelling many miles away from his home river.

Food for trout seems easier to find in the sea than in the river, and the smolt grows fast and becomes a *whitling* or *finnock*, local names which mean a little white fellow. At this stage he may come back for a spell to his own river or a neighbouring one, but in a few weeks or months he is away to sea again and stays there until he has become a fully-fledged sea trout with silvery sides and shiny, metallic blue back. He is a stout and active fish when he comes back to his own river to breed, quite different from the brown trout which stayed at home in fresh water. The male and female sea trout make their way far up the rivers in autumn and find beds of gravel in shallow places. The females plough furrows in the gravel with their powerful tails and lay eggs there. The male swims near excitedly, keeping off such would-be marauders as other trout or eels. Then he fertilizes the eggs in the

20

Young trout

furrow with *milt* from his own body; afterwards the gravel is pulled over the eggs and they lie there till hatching time in January. The breeding season of fish is usually known as the spawning time and the sea trout come back to their own river each year to spawn, and then return for another period of feeding in the sea.

The sea trout of different rivers coming down to English and Scottish coasts tend to vary in the actual times of the year at which they *run* up the rivers before spawning. And in the same river there are some sea trout which do not behave like their fellows. They may spend several months in the river before or after spawning, and some may run up and back again within a few days.

A sea trout remaining in fresh water loses the fine fat condition he had in the sea and his skin loses its silveriness. If he were to become land-locked and be prevented from returning to the sea he would eventually follow much the same life as a brown trout which had never been away, and he would begin to look more like a brown trout.

The slob trout of the estuaries may be brown trout which have descended the rivers and taken to life in the brackish, tidal water, or they may be sea trout which have given up their migratory habit; or they may be made up of both kinds. Who knows? The point is that the environment of the estuary has turned them into a certain type, something between the sea trout and the brown trout.

Sea trout are placed in the same class as salmon by the law of Scotland, so if you caught one in a Scottish river it would be no good your telling the river bailiff that sea trout and brown trout were but different races of the same species. On this point the law and the science of zoology do not agree. The sea trout is reserved for those

21

*Fishing without
a license. A heron*

who own or pay rent for the fishing. And, as are salmon, these fine silvery fish with the pale pink flesh are caught with rod and line in the rivers and with various kinds of nets in the estuaries, at a given season of the year, which may be from February to September or some time within these months.

You may wonder how so much has been learned of the life history of the sea trout. Much has become known by marking them in the whitling stage and recording details of the fish at the time of capture. The mark consists of a tiny metal tab fastened into the dorsal fin (that is the large one on top of the back) by fine silver wire. This does not seem to cause the fish any harm or discomfort as it swims on its way through life. Then it may be caught again a few days, months or years later, and by referring to the earlier record, the marker knows something at least of how far the fish has travelled, whether it has come back to its own river and how much it has grown in the meantime. Whether for birds, fish or other animals, marking is one of the best methods in the hands of the scientist for studying migrations and some other details of life history.

The Salmon

The salmon is a fish which has interested and puzzled mankind for thousands of years, and even to-day, after years of research by men in Britain and Scandinavia, the salmon holds its secrets. Few fish attract our attention as this one does: have you ever stood by a weir, rapids or falls in a river up which the salmon run? If you have, I should guess that you were not the only one standing there. There is something fascinating in watching these bold, silvery fish thrusting forwards up the river against the rush of water, leaping from the foam to surmount such obstacles as a weir or falls. Many times have I seen the people of a village gathered on the banks to watch the salmon run.

This happens at known seasons in each river and usually after heavy rain when the rivers are in spate. A roar of waters, the dark sky, the fish gleaming as they leap and the silent people watching. Where have the fish come from, where are they going and why? Some of it can be told, but much more is unknown.

The salmon is a member of the same family as the sea trout and brown trout, and is one of those fish which can live in either fresh or salt water. But it is no matter of chance whether the salmon is in river or sea and it does not take to a life in the brackish water of estuaries as trout may do.

The eggs hatch in the *redds* or furrows of gravel made by the female fish in various suitable places in rivers. The *alevins* or very young salmon do not move far from the protection of the gravel until they become *parr* at a few weeks old, when they distribute themselves about the river. They become smolts at two or three years old and then grow silvery and move towards the sea. So far their life history is much the same as that of the sea trout, but the salmon smolts do not stay about the estuary or the sea immediately offshore. They move suddenly and swiftly and go far out into deep water.

Alevins, or newly hatched salmon

That is the last we know of them for a year or two. They are not caught accidentally in nets set for other fish and are not seen feeding at any particular place in the sea. They disappear from our knowledge altogether. And then, at a season which is the same each year for any one part of the coast, the young salmon come back in large numbers. The name *grilse* is given to these fish which are not yet fully grown up.

Grilse of the East Coast appear in the spring and run up the rivers to spawn fairly early in the autumn. Those of the West Coast of Scotland run about the middle of July and are round the shores for only the short period of a fortnight or so. This is a time when much

24

rain begins to fall in the Highlands and the rivers are full and ready for the fish. Should rain be scarce and the rivers very low the grilse may be kept waiting in the bays and sea lochs.

The grilse return to sea after spawning and feed and grow, but again we do not know where they go. It has been suggested that their feeding ground is somewhere in the North Atlantic or in the Arctic Ocean.

Salmon return to different rivers at different times, and in some rivers there are two or more runs of salmon in the year. Spawning takes place from September to January by these successive runs of fish, and as rivers alter in depth and speed with the seasons, it is found that in rivers where there are several runs, all the suitable gravelly places are used as redds.

Early running fish go high up the river, the late runs occupy the lower beds and are not long in the fresh water before returning to the sea. Salmon which make very long journeys up the rivers to the breeding ground are much more exhausted than

Salmon in the spawning beds

those making short ones. Most of the far-running fish die after their first spawning and, as the net fishing is so well organized on the East Coast of Britain, few salmon spawn more than once. West Coast salmon may breed four or even five times, but not more. Thirteen years has been given as the greatest age which a salmon can reach.

It is believed that the various runs of fish are separate races of salmon and that there is no mixing between them at the breeding time, though the great shoals may mix when feeding in the sea. The salmon as a species seems to be split up into a large number of races which do not interbreed, for the smolts marked in a river as they are leaving for the sea are never retaken as grilse or adult salmon in any other river than that in which they were born, though they have been retaken from coastal nets many hundreds of miles from their home river. That is another thing we do not know—how the fish find their way back unerringly to the river of their birth.

Once a salmon is in the sea, that is, after it has left the river as a smolt, it never feeds again in fresh water. The salmon stop feeding as they approach the estuaries and their throat begins to close. Therefore, the whole of the energy required for the journey to the spawning beds, for spawning itself and for the return to the sea, comes from that stored in the body of the fish. They come to the rivers in fine, fat condition and may return as very thin, poor fish which are known as *kelts*.

It is difficult for us who like our food little and often (or perhaps not so little!) to understand why a fish should exchange a life of plenty for one of starvation. This is what some salmon do: they come into the river several months before they are ready to breed and do not

An otter with a kelt

26

Salmon netting on the Torridge estuary

seem to make a determined journey up to the spawning beds as do the runs of fish bent on breeding. As they are neither travelling nor breeding they lose weight but slowly, yet none the less surely, and, as far as we can see, pointlessly. Indeed, the salmon is a fish of much mystery.

Catching salmon is a seasonal industry in Britain. Nets of several kinds are used to take the fish from the sea. The Tweed Estuary is a place where you may see *sweep* nets being used for most of the year. Flat-bottomed, high-prowed cobles are rowed out from the shore, one end of the long sweep net being made fast ashore and the rest of it falling astern from where it is piled in the coble. The coble takes a circular sweep and comes back to where it started, all the net except the two ends being now in the water along the path taken by the coble. The men pull in on the two ends of the long net and any fish that were within the circle made by the coble are caught in its meshes. The men row out the net and pull it in again many times a day, every day but Sunday, in good weather and bad.

4-2

Bag nets are set along the coasts outside the estuaries. Seen from above, these nets are shaped like an arrow, the barb being a triangular bag net or trap, and the shaft is the *leader*. The leader is just a long length of net designed to turn the fish from their course. If the salmon does come against the leader, he is more inclined to turn seaward than landward and he goes alongside the leader in an effort to get round it, and then finds he has swum into this great netting bag. Some salmon undoubtedly get out of the bag, but most of them swim round inside and do not find the long slit at the head of the leader through which they came.

Stake nets of large mesh which catch the fish by the gills, as herrings are caught in a drift net, are also set in large estuaries such as those of the Solway and the Severn. But all are out of action on Sunday when the salmon goes free and is able to run up the rivers.

Salmon fishing in fresh water is mostly done by rod and line as a sport and not as a commercial fishery. Nevertheless, the well-known coracle men of the River Teify in Wales use their frail craft for taking salmon from the traps they set in the river.

The salmon is a *royal* fish and all salmon fishing was originally the property of the king. Kings of long ago made grants of the fishing to some of the nobles and landowners, so that nowadays even salmon fishing in the sea has to be leased from either the Crown or the owner of the coast. Rents are high and the numbers of fish caught may vary greatly, so no wonder the price of salmon in the shops is always high.

The Life Story of the Eel

I have described the habits of the salmon and the sea trout in changing from fresh water to salt and back again in order to lay their eggs in the oxygen-laden water high up the rivers. The common eel, which may be found as far away from the sea as the middle of England, does

An eel

the opposite. Its life history is one of the most interesting stories unravelled by zoological scientists. Dr Johannes Schmidt, a Dane, was the man who solved the mystery; he traversed the oceans of the world in his research ship *Dana*, gradually fitting together his facts into a story now known to be the truthful history of the eel.

Those eels we find under stones or in the mud of tiny streams were hatched thousands of miles away in a sea which always seems to me one of the dread and mysterious parts of the earth's surface—the Sargasso Sea near the West Indies. Deep down in that warm, calm, weed-covered sea, shunned with fear by the old sailing captains, the eels hatch from the eggs into little leaf-like creatures. These begin to swim, millions and millions of them, slowly but persistently, east-wards. They take two or three years over this great journey, feeding as they go and growing to a length of about two and a half inches by the time they reach our shores. It is at this time they change their

Gulls and elvers

29

shape and become just little eels, or *elvers* as they are usually called. The elvers swarm up the rivers, and millers who use water wheels to drive their mills sometimes have trouble clearing the little fish from the lade.

Eel catchers are fishermen, but the boats they use are of the nature of punts, and they do not take to the sea. They just set eel traps in the rivers when the hordes of eels are on passage and the fish caught are cooked and sold as jellied eels.

The elvers are not content merely to stay in the rivers and smaller streams which run into them, but colonize the whole countryside so that hardly a pond is without its eels. They leave the streams and wriggle through the grass in order to do this. There they stay feeding for five or six years until a new restlessness comes upon them: again they wriggle away from the ponds across the fields or down ditches until they reach stream or river, and on and on downwards until the sea is reached. That in itself may be a mighty journey for a small fish, but this is only the beginning of the three thousand miles yet to be covered, back to the warm weediness of the Sargasso Sea. The eel becomes silvery when it reaches the sea, its eyes enlarge and its head grows sharper; and by the time the fish arrive at their breeding ground the spawn is ripe inside them. They lay their eggs and die.

The eels of America are a slightly different species from our European eel, and they become elvers a year earlier than ours. And yet they also breed in the Sargasso Sea not far from the home of the European eel. Their journey to the eastern American seaboard is shorter than that of their cousins to western Europe, a year shorter we might say.

We see that the eels make two long journeys in their life, spawn once and die. Salmon and sea trout do not normally make such long journeys, and live to breed several times. But the sea trout of the Polish Vistula make a very long run up that river from the Baltic Sea and are thought to spawn only once. Similarly, the closely related salmon of the American Pacific coast; those that make very long journeys to spawn at the head of the Alaskan rivers never return to the sea. The fish have so much energy to expend: if it is used in making a long journey they can breed but once; if short journeys only are necessary, as in the rivers of the West Coast of Scotland, then the fish may come and go and breed several times.

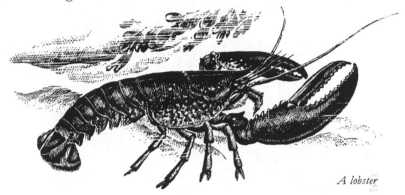

A lobster

THE FISHING AT THE SEA'S EDGE

LOBSTERS AND CRABS

THERE is no set season for catching shellfish, but perhaps more are eaten in summer than in winter. Lobsters and crabs are caught in most places round our shores, and though the method is broadly the same everywhere, there are many differences of detail. The fisherman makes a cage-like basket, the entrance to which appears fairly large from outside, but it is small and difficult for the lobster to find once he is inside. These crab and lobster traps are called pots in England and creels in Scotland. They vary much in

31

design. Those of southern England are almost circular and made of withies; northern Scottish are flat and rectangular on the bottom with semi-circular hoops of hazel, over which is spread strong string netting; those of Brittany are cylindrical, made of cane and fitted with a small open-ended cylinder set at right angles to the main one, and through which the lobster crawls.

This is a fact you will notice as you go about the country and see tasks done by hand—the men of different places have the same idea in the tools of their craft, but there will be strongly marked differences in the details of manufacture. I have just mentioned three kinds of lobster creels, but you will notice differences from place to place in the design of boats as well, in bow and stern, in oars and rowlocks or thole pins. These differences in small boats, the yawls of Devon and Yarmouth, the cobles of Northumberland, the fifies, zulus and skaffas of eastern Scotland, the yollies of Shetland, are all for some purpose connected with the type of sea on which they have to work, whether it is very shallow as off Yarmouth or Northumberland, or deep and oceanic as off Devon and Cornwall and about the Shetlands. You may see differences on farms in various parts of Britain in the designs of wagons, scythes, devices for tying cows and so on.

But to come back to catching these lobsters and crabs which inhabit the fairly shallow and weedy parts of the coastal seas. The fisherman baits his creels or pots with a piece of fish, salty fish for preference, tied inside the basket where the lobster cannot reach it unless he goes inside. Have you looked at a lobster and noticed how bristly with feelers, claws and so on is his fore end? It might well be wondered how he could get into the fairly small hole of the creel nose first with all that paraphernalia round his face. Well, if he cannot get in easily head first he goes backwards. A lobster has a fan-like tail of hard plates by which he pulls himself through the water backwards. If you have the chance to watch them swimming like this in an aquarium you will see the several organs about their face do not get in their way at all. They can walk forward easily and normally find their food that way. Crabwise means going sideways and that is how a crab gets along and is able to walk into the hole in a creel.

The lobster fisherman loads his boat high with creels, each of which is weighted by a stone to keep it on the bottom of the sea, and rows or sails forth to his chosen grounds. Each creel also has a length of thin rope tied to it, a few fathoms longer than the depth of the sea where the creel is *shot*, and the end of the rope is loaded with corks which keep it at the surface of the water, so that the fisherman can see where his creels are and is able to pull them up when he goes to them next day. Small cork floats are not so common on coasts where the sea is very shallow for a long way out: a large slab of cork or piece of wood is used then, and a flag on a stick is fastened in the top, by which means the fisherman can see the position of his pots from a distance of a mile or two.

The strong claws of the blue-black lobsters are tied after they are taken out of the trap and in this live but fettered state they are sent to the market. Only during boiling does the lobster turn bright red. Sometimes you may see a mother lobster in a trap with a large number of eggs sticking to her legs; she should be put back in the sea then, because if she is taken it is not only her life which is lost but that of all the eggs as well. When laying these little round eggs the lobster lies on her back, and as they leave her body they fall among her numerous legs, where they easily stick, and she carries them about until they hatch.

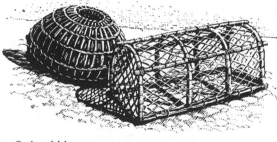

Crab and lobster pots

5

The lobster fisherman sees more of that part of the sea with which you are familiar from your own hours spent exploring the sands and rocky shores. He also sees the rock pools with their brilliant colouring and varied life of seaweeds, limpets, sea anemones and tiny glistening fish; he too looks down into that dim forest of the tangle and thongweed a few yards out from the shore, where starfish lie on the little clearings of sand and bristly sea urchins hang on the fronds of the tangle.

Turnstones and mussels on a rock

Mussels and Cockles, Alive, Alive-O

Mussels, cockles, oysters, clams and scallops are members of a group of shellfish known as the bivalves. All these are sought for food, though the first three are most commonly fished.

Mussels are gathered from the large beds of them which are to be seen in river estuaries and the mouths of streams at low tide; they are used more for bait by fishermen now than for human food, though mussel soup is reckoned very good.

34

Oysters lie in the mud well below low-tide mark and are dredged up from the beds. These beds are marked by stakes on the Essex coast near Colchester where many oysters are gathered, and the fishermen pay rent for marked areas just as a farmer may pay rent for his fields. The oysters are sent alive in their shells to London and elsewhere, mainly to the large hotels.

Cockles lie bedded in the sand just above and round about the low-tide mark. They are fished on the Essex coast also, and Burnham-on-Crouch is the centre for them. The boats, which are of a tubby, flat-bottomed type, go forth on the ebb of the tide to a distance of two or three miles from shore. The sea is shallow there and it is not long before the boats are dry and sitting on the sand. Out jump the fishers and work as hard as they can digging the cockles from the sand and filling them into baskets which are emptied into the boats; they have to work fast for they have not more than an hour or two before the tide comes in again. They come home on the flow of the tide which has now refloated the boats. There are large tanks and boilers on shore where the cockles are washed free from sand and boiled. Then they are placed on large riddles to part them from the shells which have opened wide in the boiling, and the bright yellow cockles, now ready to eat, are sent to London, where large quantities are sold in working-class districts.

Cockles

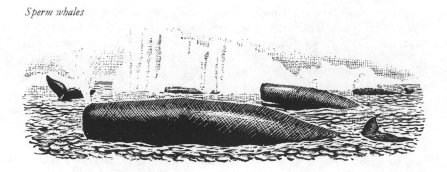

Sperm whales

THE WARM-BLOODED BEASTS OF THE SEA

THE GREAT WHALES

THE whales are not fish but warm-blooded animals that feed
their young with milk. It is not surprising that, as their whole
life is spent cruising the oceans of the world, they should be
roughly fish-shaped, but if you ever get the chance of seeing a whale
you will notice one big difference in the tail from the shape of a fish.
Fishes' tails are vertical, the tails of whales, dolphins and porpoises
are horizontal.

The zoologist and the whaling man divide whales into two main
groups—those that have teeth and those having horny, baleen plates
instead. Toothed whales capture such animals as giant squids for food
and some are wholly carnivorous, like the killer whales, which will
attack any of the larger animals of the sea. The true killer whales are
not common round British coasts, but during the summer of 1940

36

I passed a school of four of them in my motor launch a few miles out in the Minch near my home on the Isle of Tanera. I recognized them —and especially the bull whale—by the shape of the immense, spiky fin sticking up from the animal's back. The sperm whale, the one with the great blunt head and comparatively small lower jaw, is also a toothed whale.

The baleen whales live on very small animals such as the prawn-like 'krill' which I mentioned in the beginning of this book. The blue whale or Sibbald's rorqual, the largest animal in the world, swims open-mouthed, gathering krill along the surface of seas near the Antarctic Circle. The great mouth closes on the hordes of little prawns engulfed therein, the whale's tongue is inflated, blown up large as you might suddenly blow up a balloon, and this presses the water through the fringed baleen plates which hold the krill. Then the whale swallows them down a throat hardly large enough to take a man's arm. Think of it! The blue whale may reach a length of a hundred feet and weigh a hundred and fifty tons—twenty times as much as an elephant!

Whaling has a history of nearly a thousand years and it is rather an unhappy story of man taking more from the oceans than he should. At the same time it is a stirring story of bravery, hardship and endurance. The classic tale of whaling is *Moby Dick*, by Herman Melville, who describes the early nineteenth-century fishery for sperm whales which was based on the eastern American harbour of Nantucket. But long before that Scandinavian, Dutch, British and Portuguese ships were whaling in the North Atlantic Ocean for right whales, humpbacks and finners, and had seriously lessened the number of whales to be caught there. The sperm-whale fishery was followed in all the oceans except the Antarctic and it is only within the last twenty years that the great sanctuary of whales provided by the Antarctic Ocean has been invaded.

In the old days the whaling ships went under sail only. That meant

much slower progress about the oceans, and as the ships were not as large as steam ships they could not take on board the oil of so many whales at each voyage. But the actual hunting of the whale was done from small row-boats or dories lowered from the ship. The men rowed their hardest until they came near the whale and then the harpooner in the bows threw a long barbed spear or harpoon, to the end of which was attached a great length of line. The harpoon stuck in the whale's body and away went the whale with a wild threshing of its tail. Often the dories were upset, or, if all went well, the dory would be pulled for several miles before the whale became exhausted. The whaling ship would then come up and the great beast would be lashed alongside, where the men could work on it, removing the spermaceti oil from the head if it were a sperm whale, and the blubber from the body.

That is the main product obtained from whales, the blubber or thick blanket of soft fat which surrounds the whale's body underneath the skin. I use the word 'blanket' because it describes one of the uses of the blubber to the whale—it keeps him warm as he swims through the cold oceans. The old whaling may not have destroyed the stocks of whales as quickly as the modern methods tend to do, but it was very wasteful. When the blubber and spermaceti were removed all that immense carcass was let go from the ship's side and became food for sharks and crowds of sea birds.

Whaling in the northern oceans, particularly in the Atlantic, has almost ceased because the stocks of whales have grown so small. No more do wooden ships set forth from Dundee for Arctic waters, and the Shetland and Orkney Islands are no longer whaling bases as in olden days. Captain Scott's ship, *Terra Nova*, was a Dundee whaler, and even I, who am counted still a young man, can remember seeing a Norwegian whaler in one of the northern firths of Shetland.

When the numbers of whales become so low that it is not profitable to hunt them any more, there is this thought with which to comfort ourselves: there is the possibility that the great beasts which remain will be left in peace and will have time to breed and increase their numbers. You may know that I have lived on several tiny islands off the West Coast of Scotland and it has been part of my work to watch the life of the sea and the coasts; not many days would pass without my seeing at least one whale, so we may hope they are not yet in danger of extinction.

Times have changed. The whalers of to-day are much larger ships, made of iron and steam-driven. Norway and Britain have the largest fleet of whaling ships and they have been responsible for developing the whale fishery of the Antarctic Ocean. Their profits were very large at the beginning and other seafaring nations came to take their toll.

Large ships of 15,000 tons are equipped as floating factories and small ships of the size of trawlers are used in conjunction with these as whale catchers. The small boats have a harpoon gun in the bows fired by a powerful cartridge, not a man who could but throw with the strength and skill of his own arm. Whale catching has become much surer, but the numbers of whales are decreasing. The catchers are fast little ships and they return with the whale in tow to the factory ship or to a base on shore like that of South Georgia, a good way south of South America.

The whale is flensed or skinned of its blubber at the base and the rest of the carcass is cooked in huge vats and dried to form feeding stuffs for cows, pigs and hens here at home. The blubber is melted down and the clear oil resulting from this process is used at home for

Stripping the blubber at a whaling station

several purposes, particularly the manufacture of margarine and soap, but another of the uses is as an ingredient of sheep dip, in which it is thought to provide a waterproof film to the wool fibres of the fleece.

Antarctic whaling takes place from October to March, that is, in the summer season of the southern hemisphere. The whales themselves inhabit the warmer waters of the Indian and Pacific Oceans during the southern winter.

I have mentioned the great increase of the Antarctic whale fishery and its effect of decreasing the numbers of whales. Were all the nations concerned to hunt the animals without regard to numbers or to the claims of each other, it would soon become unprofitable to go that great distance with big ships and expensive gear. Then the whales would either gradually increase again or possibly become extinct. It is known that if animals are reduced to very low numbers they tend to stop breeding and do not increase again.

But one thing would be certain for the business men who own the whaling ships: their source of profit would be gone; and though you and I might wish to regulate the numbers and ages of whales caught in order to reduce cruelty and for love of the great creatures, we must be glad that those who are thinking only of safeguarding profits must take care of the stocks of whales as well. The governments of many countries have made an agreement restricting the capture of whales. This restriction is to act in three ways—large areas of ocean are to be left untouched as sanctuaries, whaling is to take place during a three months' season only in the year and no blue whales below seventy feet and fin whales under fifty-five feet are to be caught, nor any cows with calves along with them.

Civilized countries are trying to take greater care of their fisheries, because it is realized that if we overfish certain parts of the sea now, there will be few or no fish for the generations of people who will follow us. That care is exercised in several ways as you will read in the last chapter of this book.

Seals, North and South

The whales were once land-going animals, but for many millions of years now they have kept entirely to the sea. Their fore legs have

A common seal

turned into flippers showing no separate claws and their hind legs have outwardly disappeared altogether. If they should be stranded ashore they die, being pressed to death by their own immense weight.

Seals are also animals of the sea, but they still come on shore to rest and to have their young ones. Their hands are webbed, but the fingers are separate, each with its own claw. The hind legs are also there, extending behind the body, but they are not used by the true seals when moving on land. Sea lions come a little nearer to an existence on shore, for their hind legs are placed under the body and can be used more or less as the legs of other four-footed animals.

It is difficult for us to understand the behaviour of the whales in the same way we do that of dogs and cats because the life of the whale is so far removed from our own, but most of us know sea lions and have had the wish to keep them as pets. They are as intelligent as a dog and even more full of fun. Some seals are almost as clever as the sea lions and they too are fond of a romp whether in the sea or ashore. They have bonny faces with dark, kindly eyes; our feelings towards them are warm and we think of them as creatures not far removed from ourselves.

Nevertheless, seals are hunted by man; there are extensive seal fisheries in both the northern and southern hemispheres. There have been examples of human greed in taking too many, just as we saw was occurring in the whale fisheries, and there are also examples of great care being taken to preserve the stocks of seals. Some seal fisheries are well conducted and some are wasteful, and though deep down in our hearts we may regret these beautiful animals being killed at all, the best thing to do is to use our influence as far as we can towards carefully controlled fishing and non-wasteful methods.

The harp seal and bladder-nose seal of the Arctic and North Atlantic Oceans have their single pups on the ice floes drifting southwards off the Labrador coast in March. These fluffy, white-coated pups provide a fur for coats much liked by some fashionable people. Ten thousand men go forth with the sealing fleet on 12 March each year from St John's, Newfoundland. They face great hardship and danger, leaping about the ice floes with their long poles in search of the seal pups, and the slaughter of three hundred thousand baby seals is rather horrible. Sometimes a batch of skins is lost entirely through an ice

Pup of the
bladder-nosed seal

6-2

floe breaking up and no use is made of the carcasses after the removal of the skin. This is one of the wasteful seal fisheries.

The Russians are now fishing adult seals off their Arctic coast, using every part of the animal for leather, oil or food. Similarly, among the group of islands round the Antarctic whaling station of South Georgia, the elephant seals (very large and rather unintelligent) are taken when they are ashore in the numerous bays. The coasts are divided into four sections, only one section being hunted each year, and then only bulls are taken. Thus the stock of elephant seals is increasing, and any sorrow we may feel for the individual seals killed

Elephant seals

is overweighed by our gladness in knowing that the total numbers are growing larger.

The story of the Alaskan fur seal has often been told. American, Japanese and Russian sealers had hunted these fine animals in the Aleutian chain of islands near the Behring Straits until there were only ten thousand seals left in all that vast area. The United States Government then protected them very closely, until a stock of over a

44

million had been built up. No private hunters are allowed in the seal islands, all hunting being done by the government at the time when the seals come ashore to breed. They take only bulls of four years of age and over. The seal fishery is now profitable and the animals are saved from extinction. The United States Government provides a patrol cruiser to escort the great herd of fur seals on their migration from the feeding grounds off the northern Californian coast up the west coast of America and Canada to the breeding grounds at the Pribiloff Islands. The fur seals are in fine, fat condition as they go northwards and it is necessary to protect them from ships making an attempt to poach them.

Britain has no seal fishery now, though years ago men from the Outer Hebrides used to go to the remote islets of Hasgeir and North Rona in the Atlantic Ocean to kill Atlantic grey seals. Their fishery was intensely wasteful, for they went in small sailing boats on but one occasion in the breeding season, when the autumn gales allowed, and they killed bulls, cows and calves for their skins and oil. Happily, the Government of Britain acted in time and made a law protecting these seals from any hunting during the breeding season from 1 August to 1 December. These fine seals, probably the rarest kind in the world, have now increased, but the need to care for them has not yet passed. It has been my good fortune to live with these seals on North Rona throughout a breeding season, and it was a wonderful experience to see five thousand of them ashore at once. But I had to remember that here were about half of the world's stock of Atlantic seals.

All seal fisheries need careful regulation because the habit of many species of seal is to gather in large numbers at chosen breeding grounds. The animals come ashore in fat condition at these few places and starve for several weeks at the breeding season. These large congregations can be so easily attacked ashore and the young seals are helpless. A greater understanding of the life histories of the animals will lead to their greater care in the future.

Long line fishing

THE FISHERIES OF THE SEAS

THE INSHORE FISHERIES

THERE was a time when all sea fishing was *inshore*, fishing done in small boats which did not go more than ten to fifteen miles from shore. That was before larger ships were organized to fish with modern trawl nets. But inshore fishing continues from hundreds of small villages dotted round the coasts of Britain. It is of special importance to the country in several ways; the fish caught is much fresher than that marketed from the big trawler ports, for the fish is caught in the night time and is marketed the following morning: this fishery means that a large number of men is being trained to the sea and, as the boats are usually owned by families of fisher folk themselves, it means the fishing villages are peopled by a strongly inde-

46

pendent race. Their determination to fish in fair weather or foul and to carry on in their own way, despite the difficulties of selling their fish as profitably as the trawling companies, calls forth our admiration.

Many of the fishing villages had no harbours or piers years ago and the boats were without engines. This meant an immense amount of hard labour hauling up the boats and taking them down to sea again. Men and women together hauled on the wheeled bogies which were run under the boats while they were yet afloat. The women of fishing villages which I know on the East Coast of Scotland are particularly big and strong, and so they needed to be, for when the fishing boats—fifies, zulus and skaffas—were got down to the sea, they would put their menfolk aboard them dry-foot by carrying them on their backs through the surf. Those were the days before waist-high rubber boots.

The women's work did not end with this heavy labour at the shore. The inshore fishermen fish mostly with lines and hooks, though they may leave this kind of fishing alone when the herring season comes to their stretch of coast; then they use drift nets instead. *Small line* fishing means that these thirty- to forty-foot boats will each have a crew of three or four and two lines of eight hundred hooks each are managed by each man. The hooks hang from the line on about two feet of twisted gut called a *snood*. Each hook is baited with a mussel.

The fishermen gather large stocks of mussels and plant them on gravelly places in the estuaries or where a stream comes down to the sea. The mussels take hold, grow large and increase. It is the women's task to bait the hooks, and often enough they have the mussels to fetch from the beds or scalps, though nowadays there is an increasing tendency for a man in the village who has a motor lorry to gather enough mussels for the whole village and carry them to the doors.

Have you ever seen fishermen's wives and daughters shelling mussels and baiting hooks? It is not a very easy or pleasant job, for the shells are sharp and could easily cause a nasty cut to the fingers. A knife is pushed into the mussel where the two sides of the shell

47

meet, a quick pull along between the sharp edges, the knife is turned at right angles, in goes a thumb and the mussel is open. The flesh is cleared from each shell by another two scoops of the short knife and the white and orange-coloured shellfish is nipped free. The mussels are dropped into salt water for a little time to toughen them and then, in baiting the hooks, the barbed point is passed through the gristly bit of the mussel and the stringy ends are deftly wrapped round the shank of the hook and slipped over the barb again. This makes a tight job.

A small line with its eight hundred hooks attached to it is about a quarter of a mile long, so you can imagine how easily it could get into a horrible, tangled mess. The womenfolk who bait the hooks show great skill in laying the line into a basket neatly coiled with all the hooks coming to one side. When the fishermen come to their chosen fishing ground, the two lines carried by each man are shot, one after another, and canvas buoys hold the line at the right depth for fishing. The men wait then for two hours or longer to let the lines *fish*. Then comes the hauling in: the hooks may have caught nothing or there may be a fish on nearly every hook. It is the luck of the game.

Haddock, whiting, codling: these are the three commonest fish caught by inshore men on small lines. Sometimes big cod come inboard as well when the lines are hauled in, and it must be annoying when the fisherman finds starfish on the hooks, for not only are they worthless in themselves but they have taken up a hook which might have held a haddock. Some of the hooks may have caught dogfish

A dogfish

which are almost worthless to the inshore fisherman except that they may be used for bait in lobster creels. The dogfish also have a disconcerting habit of snatching at the fish on the hooks and spoiling them for sale.

The boat heads for home as soon as possible after the lines are in. The men gut and sort the fish meanwhile, so that when harbour is reached no time is lost in getting the fish into the auction and away to the market.

These small inshore boats change their type of fishing with the season. Small lines may be laid aside to go drift netting for herring or a *seine* net may be used for flat fish. The seine net originated in Denmark and is very popular now with inshore fishermen because its use means no lines to bait every day. A seine net consists of a conical bag where the fish are held, on each side of which are thirty-five yards of plain netting. At the end of each wing is a strong line or *warp* about a mile long. The fisherman drops the free end of the warp overboard on a buoy: he goes ahead for a mile, turns sharply and runs out the net on this new course; then he turns sharply again, letting out the other warp from the end attached to the net, and sails back to where he started. He takes up the two free ends of the warps and hauls in slowly. The fish coming against the wings of the net tend to be turned towards the end of the bag and are caught.

Flat fish, mainly flounders, may be caught in shallow water where the bottom is sandy by spearing them from the stern of a row-boat. This easy kind of fishing can be done only when the water is quite calm, because if there is much ripple the reflection of light from the water prevents the bottom being seen clearly enough to use the spear.

The inshore men may go to the cod banks when the fish congregate there to spawn. They will then use hand lines and *jig* for the cod, that is, jerk the lines up and down over the side of the boat. At the business end of the line is a very cunning and rather horrible fish-catching device called a 'murderer' or 'ripper'. A polished, fish-shaped piece

Northern Ireland 'hand-liners'

of metal has a large hook hanging a few inches below it: the cod comes at this lure, which jerks upward and the hook enters under his chin.

Hand lines are also used on the West Coast, from Land's End to Cape Wrath, to catch pollack or lythe as they are called in Scotland. These large fish of from four to fourteen pounds in weight haunt the weed-covered rocks off the outer shores. Imitation sand eels made of rubber with a hook in the tail are used as bait. The boat moves along slowly and the rubber eel spins merrily, luring the fish from the shelter of the tangle. Pollack are caught mainly in summer time, and as they keep but poorly and are not reckoned very appetizing fish, they are eaten in the neighbourhood where they are caught and not sent away to the markets.

Hard as is his life at sea, the inshore fisherman is always busy ashore making his gear and mending nets. His skill is as varied as that of the farmer, and, like him, his work is never done. If it is hard for a towns-man to become a successful farmer, it is still harder for anyone not born to it to become an inshore fisherman. That is one reason why it would never do for the government of the country to let the inshore

Off to the trawling grounds

fisheries lapse in competition with the more highly organized trawl fisheries. Are not these the men who man the lifeboats, and never fail a ship in distress?

Trawlers of the Dogger and of the Deep Seas

Trawling, or catching fish by dragging a large bag of a net behind a ship, is no new thing. There was trawling in the Straits of Dover and in the Thames Estuary as far back as the fourteenth century, and even in those days the line fishermen addressed a petition to the king, asking that this method of fishing should be stopped because it would clear all the fish from the fishing grounds. The population of Britain then was not much more than a million souls and transport of fresh sea fish to inland districts was impossible, so the amount of fish taken by trawlers at that time must have been very small. There are fifty million people to-day and fresh fish can be bought in any town in the country. Where does all this fish come from, and how has it become possible to catch so much?

The command of steam as a source of power allowed industries to develop in British towns, and that meant a rapid increase in population during the first half of the nineteenth century. Steam was used on land long before it was used in ships, so the sailing trawlers of those days found a ready market in the industrial towns for all they could catch. They could then have sold far more than they were able to catch by the methods they were using at that time. Any industry finding itself in that position attracts the cleverness and inventiveness of men's minds, and new methods and tools come into use to enable the industry to meet the demand for its products.

First of all, the manufacture of ice allowed the fish caught to be preserved in fresh condition at sea, and the sailing trawlers could stay a longer time on the fishing ground; less time was wasted going to and from port. Then steam engines were used in trawlers, which meant quicker journeys. Lastly, the invention of the enormous *otter trawl*, which entirely replaced the small *beam trawl*, allowed of great catches being made. This net could never have been used by the man power of the small ships of earlier days; a steam winch is necessary for hauling it aboard. A beam trawl net was kept open by a beam of wood stretched across its mouth. An otter trawl is kept open by the passage of water through slatted kites of wood called 'otters' fitted one at each side of the net.

This development of speed and capacity caused the fishermen to go farther afield. All the central area of the North Sea was untouched and it proved to be an extremely rich fishing ground with exactly the right kind of sandy bottom for trawling. Plaice and soles in abundance, turbot and haddocks; the fishing was profitable and intense, but before the war of 1914 there were signs that the North Sea was being overfished and profits dropped.

The trawl alongside

The trawlers of Fleetwood and Milford Haven were similarly fishing hard on the West Coast grounds and were overdoing it. They were the first ones to move farther afield, and they fitted out their trawlers to fish round the Faroe Islands and as far as Iceland. Much of Britain's fish supply now comes from those waters.

The war of 1914–18 allowed the fish of the North Sea time to grow and increase their numbers, for the trawlers were minesweeping and doing other work of national defence. Immediately after the war, therefore, the trawlers of the Dogger Bank were reaping rich harvests once more, and yet again they overfished the grounds, rendering them less and less profitable.

The men of Hull followed the example of those of Fleetwood in going farther afield, but they went farther still. New trawlers were built to carry a crew of twenty-three men, ships which are far more comfortable than most of the trawlers of nearer seas. The engines are very powerful, allowing the ship to speed at a maximum of $16\frac{1}{2}$ knots, though 12 knots is the usual cruising speed under good conditions. (A knot is a speed of one sea mile an hour, and a sea mile is 6080 feet, that is, 800 feet longer than a land mile.)

These long-distance trawlers of Hull are the smartest fishing boats on the seas and they are manned for the most part by young men.

They steam northwards towards Norway, pick up a Norwegian pilot at Lödingen, thread their way for four days through the islands and fiords of that coast and come in sight of the North Cape. Here the pilot is dropped and the trawler goes on into the White Sea or farther north still to rich new fishing grounds in the neighbourhood of Bear Island.

All these trawlers are fitted with an electrical *echo-sounding* machine. Sailors are always anxious to know the depth of water below them when they are near the shore, and to measure the depth and find out what sort of bottom it is they make a *sounding* with a lead cylinder fastened to a long length of line. The lead is swung by a man standing high in the bows of the ship, and as the line is marked in half fathoms he is able to call out the depth in fathoms to the skipper. The bottom of the lead cylinder is hollow and, when it is pulled to the surface again, a little of the sea bottom is lodged in this hollow if it is of sand or mud. The good skipper is expert in judging his position from knowledge of the depth and the sample of the sea floor.

The use of the lead is a slow and laborious way of sounding. The echo-sounding apparatus gives a continuous record on a chart on the bridge of the ship of soundings made every half second. A little electric hammer is fixed to the inside of the hull of the ship below the water line. Tap-tap-tap goes the hammer continuously, the sound is carried to the floor of the sea and comes back again to the bottom of the ship as an echo. The sound of the echo is picked up by a microphone and transmitted to the instrument on the bridge. The echo will reach the ship's bottom sooner in shallow water than in deep and it is this difference in time that has allowed the development of the echo-sounder.

Well, here we are in the Arctic fishing grounds, the echo-sounder showing a gently shelving smooth bottom at a thousand feet. The trawl net is lowered into the water and about three thousand feet of warp is run off the drum, three times the depth of the water being

Untying the cod end

fished. The trawler goes ahead for perhaps two hours before the trawl is wound in. Up she comes over the side in front of the bridge and half-way up the foremast the winch draws the net until the *cod end* of the net is above the deck. Then the cod end is untied and the fish come helter skelter, flapping and slapping on to the deck—turbot and other flat fish, haddock, cod, rays and evil-looking catfish. Over goes the net for another two hours' trawl and the men, clad in warm woollens, oilskins and high sea boots, begin sorting the fish. The mate is down in the hold supervising the packing of the fish in ice, packing it with the utmost care because a fortnight may pass before they are back to port. Turbot is a high-priced fish, haddock and cod reach the tables of most people. The rays and skates, though flat and square, are unlike the true flat fish. They are allied to the sharks and are without a real bony skeleton. They are excellent food and mostly eaten by poorer people.

These trawlers will carry from a hundred and fifty to two hundred tons of fish, the total of sixty to a hundred trawls. The voyage takes three weeks—a week getting to the fishing grounds, a week fishing and a week coming home, so if you take seventy trawls as an average fishing, there are ten trawls a day. Ten trawls of two hours each do not leave the men much time to themselves while they are on the grounds. And once loaded, they are two thousand miles of northern waters away from home.

Fine men these: hardy, resolute, in charge of ship, fine machinery and gear worth £23,000: they are on top of their job.

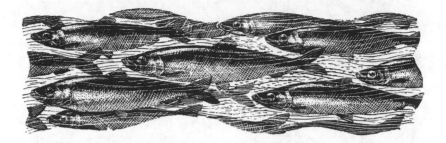

The Herring

The herring fishery must be one of the oldest in Britain and it has called forth a long tradition of ocean-going seamen round our coasts. Herrings have been an article of export from Britain since medieval times, for the Hanseatic League of Merchants of the Baltic ports, such as Danzig, began the continental trade in salt herring which has lasted until our own day.

During the eighteenth century cured herrings were exported from the West Coast of Scotland to the plantations of America and the West Indies, to be eaten by the negroes who were then slaves. Salt and red herrings were also sent to Ireland in large quantities. This very house and pier where I live on the Isle of Tanera were once the scene of a busy herring fishery. The boats or 'busses' (double S please note) that took the herring to Ireland from here came back in ballast with Irish soil, and that is one reason why my garden has deep rich soil when all around is peat and bare rock.

This small silvery fish of great beauty swarms in countless numbers round our shores at certain seasons of the year. The young fish feed a long way offshore, in the Atlantic or as far north as the Arctic Ocean, and come to the West Coast of Scotland when they are near the age for their first spawning. Herring cannot be taken on a hook, for they feed on plankton only. This food makes them fat and oily, and young herring caught before they are in spawning condition are so soft and oily that they must be got to the table as soon as possible or they will go bad. Such fish are no good for salting or curing.

The herrings migrate round our coasts from the West of Scotland, round the North Coast and gradually down the East Coasts of Scotland and England until almost the Straits of Dover. They are off Scotland in summer and Yarmouth in late autumn, and all the time they are coming nearer to spawning condition and are now considered to be in the finest firm state for eating and curing. Spawned or *spent* herring are poor food and it is wasteful to fish them then.

Drifter
riding at the nets

The herring fleet follows the herring in this clock-wise migration. The drifters and small boats such as the fifies and zulus from the Moray Firth area may be seen going down the Caledonian Canal in spring and early summer to where the fishing begins. They bring their catches to Oban and Mallaig, then to Stornoway in the Outer Hebrides, next to the well-known herring ports of Buckie, Peterhead and Fraserburgh, and lastly to Lowestoft and Yarmouth.

A drift net is about forty yards long and ten deep and the mesh is one-and-a-quarter inches. A steam drifter may carry a hundred and twenty nets, so you can work out for yourselves what length of net is being used each night. The nets are shot, buoyed by canvas and glass floats, and are left to fish for two hours or so.

The herring fishery includes the catching of pilchards and mackerel, pilchards being mainly caught off the south-western coasts. Mackerel are to be found round our shores throughout the summer and are easily caught in nets. People who live near the sea also take them on a hook dressed with a wisp of white feather, a bit of white hair from the neck of a collie dog or, as in Ireland, a few white hairs from the beard of a goat. Fishermen of the Moray Firth area catch the first mackerel with a white feather and after that use bits of the bright skin from the sides of the mackerel for baiting later hooks.

Let us go back now to the drifter's nets. It is night time and, as the whole drifter fleet is fishing in the one area, the riding lights of the little ships shine as if there were a city in the sea.

The nets are hauled in over the side of the boat by a winch, power driven in the larger drifters and worked by hand from near the stern in the small 30–40-footers. The herring gleam in the net as it leaves the water and as it comes over the side the fishermen stretch the net and give it a quick shake to dislodge the fish which are caught by the gills in the meshes. When you see how easily they shake out you wonder why they were unable to wriggle themselves free in the water. Some of the fish will be chewed in half and worthless, once more the work of dogfish which are to be found in the neighbourhood of the herring shoals. They themselves get into the meshes at times and usually cause some mending of the nets when the fishermen are ashore.

Large flocks of sea birds gather round the drifters on the fishing grounds and follow them back to port. Fallen and damaged fish are eagerly swallowed by them, and fulmar petrels may be seen picking oily fragments from the surface of the sea. Many are the fights and sudden brawls among the concourse of gulls which make far more noise than the drifter and its crew. Great black-backs, lesser black-backs, herring gulls and kittiwakes, they are all there, and if you wish to get an easy photograph of them in flight, go for a trip on a drifter; you will have endless opportunity.

A great length of net spread near the surface of the sea is in danger of being damaged by several things. A bit of floating wreckage can cause quite a big tear, but think of those large basking sharks slowly cruising along near the surface. What is the fine string of a herring net to a forty-foot monster of his strength? He goes straight through it, hardly realizing anything was in his way, and that net is just about ruined. It is unfortunate that a fish so harmless in himself should be such a source of trouble to the nets. The drifters kill these fish by ramming them whenever chance offers, but this is a wasteful practice.

The great fish has an immense liver full of oil much more valuable than cod-liver oil. But we have no boats and tackle catching these fish now and no refineries on the West Coast, off which the basking sharks are mostly seen.

If you look at a herring drifter you will see that the upper part of the hull is painted green or black and the lower part red, but at the bows there appears a narrow wedge of white between the black and the red. An empty drifter shows all this white wedge, a heavily loaded one shows none of it; so long before the fleet is back to port with its catch, it is known on shore whether the catch has been a heavy one or not.

We have seen, then, that the herring fishery moves with the herring. Ships and crews, auctioneers and buyers, the girls who do the gutting, the coopers and the packers, all move round the coast with the annual migration of the fish until the actual spawning time comes, when the fish are no longer good to eat. One of the great breeding areas is off the Lincolnshire coast and, as a result of exact knowledge gained by scientists, this area has been closed to all herring fishing at the spawning season, so that the shoals shall not be lessened for later years.

Racing to port with the catch

THE FISH AND THE PEOPLE

THE FISHING PORTS

YOU will have gathered that this great activity of fishing, which goes on every day of the year, must mean very good and careful arrangements for receiving the fish when the trawlers, drifters and line boats bring the catches to port. Most of the fifty million people in Britain have fish in one form or another at least once a week. Fish, also, easily goes bad; so apart from arrangements for the speed with which it must be got to the port and from the port to the fishmonger's slab and fish-frier's stove, the fishing ports become centres of other industries, such as that of making ice: Aberdeen alone manufactures over 120,000 tons a year, and one trawler fleet fishing from Hull uses 300,000 tons a year. Other industries are boat repairing, barrel making, rope making, manufactures of products such as fish meal, fish manure and cod-liver oil.

Let us take the great fishing port of Aberdeen as an example of a town that handles the daily catch of fish. The coming of the steam trawlers caused the townsmen to build a large tidal basin at the docks, into which the trawlers could come at any state of the tide and begin unloading their fish. Then a covered market-place was built almost all round the basin. The trawlermen themselves do some sorting of their catch aboard the ship, but a final sorting takes place in the early mornings on the concrete floors of the fish market. Fish are not only

A corner of a fish market

sorted into species or kinds, but into sizes as well, for this is important from the fishmonger's point of view. Then, at eight o'clock in the morning, auction sales of the fish begin and there is such a noise and bustle as you never heard before. The wholesale merchants who buy the fish at Aberdeen have lorries waiting to take their buyings to the railway station, where special refrigerator vans are ready to carry the fish to many parts of the country. Fish is usually packed in boxes, and the piles of empty boxes waiting at the market are as large as houses.

The wholesale merchants themselves specialize in buying certain classes of fish. One may be buying large quantities of skates and rays, which fish, as I told you earlier, are allied to the sharks and do not have true bony skeletons. The skates and rays go to the fried-fish shops in the towns and provide good and cheap food for working people. The wholesaler fillets or cuts up the fish before it is packed and thus saves transport costs. The waste materials, such as heads, tails and insides, are taken to the fish meal and manure factories. Another buyer may be bidding for haddock only. He will take these fish to his factory in the town, where he will open them and cure or smoke them to produce the delicious finnan-haddocks or 'smokies' which most of us have enjoyed at some time or other. Still another buyer will be taking cod and saithe for drying and salting in his factory. Most of this dried, salted fish is sold for export because British people are not very fond of it.

Fish livers are rich in oil containing the vitamins which help to build our bones and prevent us from catching diseases, so there are representatives of the makers of your cod-liver oil emulsions at the fish markets also. Nothing is wasted: that is the keynote of the fishing industry of to-day. Just as a farmer receives fertility in the shape of basic slag from the blast furnaces of the steel works, so does he get food for his stock and manure for the ground from fish offals. The harvest of the ocean reaches all parts of the country.

An hour or two after the fish auctions in the market everything is clean again in readiness for the next day's catch. Men in rubber boots and clogs, with high-powered water hoses, wash down the great concrete floors and remove all smelliness. And at night time there is another important man working hard—the rat-catcher. A fish market at the water's edge is a rat's idea of a perfect playground, and a rat-catcher must be kept specially to keep the numbers down so that the fish shall be untainted.

English fishing villages, which have no large town near at hand where their catches can be sold, send their fish in boxes to Billingsgate Market in London. The great difference between this place and the Aberdeen Fish Market is that at Billingsgate there is no port or fishing vessels. It is a central market collecting its fish from far and wide.

Aberdeen is a port for trawlers which catch 'white' fish. The whole of its market and organization are devoted to handling this class of fish. But there are other ports like Peterhead, Fraserburgh, Lowestoft and Yarmouth which specialize in herrings. As I have told you already, these fish are caught by smaller boats called drifters, and drifters are much more varied in type than trawlers. They bring their

catches to the herring ports and unload them on to the quay in large, round baskets. Two of these basketsful make the herring fisher's unit of measure—a *cran*— which contains about a thousand herrings. A steam drifter may bring in a catch of two hundred cran if the crew has been lucky. Once more we find auctioneers on the quay, selling herrings at a figure of three to six pounds a cran. The buyers engage large staffs of fisher lasses, who gut the herrings which are dumped into the long troughs at which they work. Again all is speed and bustle, for to whatever purpose the herring are being put, the work of preparing them must be done quickly.

Newhaven fishwife

The herring caught in summer may be canned or sold fresh, and many are split open and made into kippers or bloaters, but most of the autumn catches are salted and packed in barrels. Salt herrings are still eaten in the Highlands and Islands of Scotland, but the rest of the people of Britain do not seem to like them. The great rows and piles of barrels of salt herrings which we see at a herring port are destined for markets abroad.

I mentioned earlier that the small fishing boats carrying a crew of three or four men, which put out from the fishing villages, are often engaged on line fishing, not netting. They go out each night and are back early in the morning. The villages of Granton and Newhaven on the Firth of Forth are good examples of such villages which have a large sale for their fish near at hand. These villages require no market-place like that of Aberdeen, for the fishwives, dressed in their distinctive uniform, carry the fish in creels from door to door. The fishwives are one of the sights of Edinburgh: they are big, fine women and look extraordinarily hardy as they walk through the streets, in all weathers, with their sleeves rolled up and carrying the creel of fish on their back by a strap resting on their head.

Line-caught fish sold like this the morning after it is caught is considered to be of the finest quality, for it has spent no time on ice in a trawler's hold. As an old man said to me once—'The fire has not gone out of it.' By 'fire' he meant the freshness, flavour and goodness.

This note runs right through the fishing industry—speed. Speed in getting to the fishing grounds, still greater speed in getting back to port with the catches, speed in selling and transporting ashore, and your mother does not buy fish the day before she intends to cook it. She wastes no time between buying and cooking and she is happiest when there is none left over from the meal.

Science of the Sea

A fisherman has to live by catching fish, and unless every other fisherman fishing the same grounds will join with him in refraining from taking fish less than a given size when working a certain stretch of water, or from taking spawning fish, he must just carry on and fish, though he may know as well as anybody else that the grounds are being overfished. That is where the government of the country can take a hand and, by making a law for all, can regulate the fishing. But that is not quite the whole story, for a sea like the North Sea is bounded by many countries, all of them with a seafaring tradition. There was a time when the herring fishery was mostly British and Dutch, then it became almost wholly British, and in our own day Germany has come into the fishery, using special trawl nets for the herring instead of drift nets. Germany has also built a large fleet of trawlers which fish on equal terms with the English ships on the Dogger Bank.

Herrings show no signs of scarcity, but the white fisheries of the North Sea, in which British, French, Belgian, German, Dutch and Danish take part, are showing every sign of being overfished. The science of the sea, fostered by all governments with fishing interests, is designed to provide detailed knowledge of the life history of fishes, of their breeding and migrations, of their food through the seasons, and of the influence upon fish of currents, water temperatures and saltness. This knowledge is set forth for all to read who will, and it is knowledge which is trusted because scientists do not seek facts to bolster up their own or other people's *opinions*; they seek truth for its own sake.

The science of the sea is a larger subject than any one nation can tackle and there has come into being an International Council for the Exploration of the Sea on which fourteen nations are represented. Between them, these nations have twenty research ships busy on problems of marine life in relation to the fisheries. The aim of the Council is to learn to what extent the sea can be fished without depleting its stocks. Scarcity of fish in any one place or in any one year is no evidence that overfishing is taking place; the movements of currents and changes in temperature or saltness at that place or time may have caused the departure of the fish. Neither, and for the same reasons, is a sudden abundance to be accepted as showing there is no overfishing. Large areas of sea and the reports of many scientists must be compared in order to get a true picture.

Much of the work of a fisheries research worker is that of taking samples, samples of water from different places and different depths, samples of the sea floor, samples of fishes' stomachs and samples of

*White fish,
mostly
haddock
and cod*

the fish themselves. Where are the feeding grounds, what are the growth rates of the fish and how are the ages of the fish to be known? Examination of samples and the collection of facts which can be fitted together like the pieces of a jig-saw puzzle; that is how the true picture is built.

We saw that in studying the life history of salmon and sea trout many of the fish were marked by the research worker in order to gain information on age and movement of the fish. But the salmon family carry about with them a record of their own life history which scientists have learned to read. This record is found in the scales which cover the skin of the fish. The scales grow larger as the fish grows, and the fish grows more in summer and in periods spent in the sea; all this can be gathered from the tiny lines which can be seen on the scale under a low power of the microscope. There is a roughness at the edge of the scale at spawning time and this also can be seen as a distinct mark in the ringed lines years afterwards. So far has this skill in scale reading been developed that a worker can now state accurately how old the fish was when it went to sea, how long it spent in the sea, how long it was in the river again and how often it has spawned; the size and weight of the fish at any given time in its life can also be calculated from a knowledge of its weight and length when caught in relation to the story told by its scales.

The same knowledge is sought from other fish, but it is not always to be got from the scales. The herring shows its life history perfectly on its scales, but not so the plaice, so new pointers to this knowledge must be found. This is where the scientist can do a job better than the fisherman: there are tiny bones in the ear known as *otoliths*, and if these are taken from a plaice, cut into very thin sections and examined under the microscope, growth rings can be seen very much like those shown in the cross-section of a tree trunk, but many fewer. If two rings are very close together you know that the fish has had a lean time, if they are far apart growth has been rapid.

Studies continued over several years show that in many kinds of fish, but in herrings particularly, there are occasional

Scale of a six-year old salmon

68

years when a very large proportion of the hundreds of thousands of eggs laid by each fish survive and provide the stock which may be fished in following years. The causes of these good years have to be learnt and, when they are known, it becomes possible to forecast the scarcity or plenty of fish from year to year.

There are two sure signs of overfishing: one is if a trawler fishes a certain region for some given period of time—say a hundred hours—and gets a steadily decreasing haul of fish; the other is the proportion of young, undersized fish in the haul, or to put it in another way, a decreasing average length of the fish caught. Well-grown mature fish represent the income to be got from the sea, and as long as you take only them, the stocks will never be depleted. But when young fish are included in the catch they represent the capital of the sea, and by taking them we are lessening the chances of catching fully grown fish later on.

When governments co-operate and say no fish less than a certain length are to be landed at the ports it is possible for the stocks of fish to increase again: an example of where such action should be taken for the good of all is provided by the North Sea, the governments and

ports bordering it, and the haddock and plaice which are fished. The main way in which the young fish can be allowed to escape is by enlarging the meshes of the nets used so that more can swim through them.

Britain led the way in this enlargement of trawl meshes and other countries have since joined her, so that fishing in the North Sea may be maintained. The result has not been the much reduced profits which some people imagined; by letting the small fish escape, more even samples of larger fish have been taken and higher prices obtained.

Otolith of a plaice

69

The science of life applied to all wild stocks of animals used by man, whether whales, seals, fish, birds or buffaloes, teaches first and foremost this need for living on income and not on capital. Take the natural increase only and learn methods of thrift by which greater stocks can be maintained to provide more increase for the generations to come. This is called *conservation* of wild life and will be one of the great aims of peoples in the new world we hope to build in the future. Thus we shall be able to continue to fish and to hunt certain animals, just as we farm others and live on their increase, and we shall have no fear that man's greed will bring about the extinction of living things.

Puffin with its catch